WRITE LIKE A PRO

WRITING ABOUT ISSUES

ROGER BEUTEL AND LAUREN SPENCER

rosen publishing's
rosen central

New York

Published in 2012 by The Rosen Publishing Group, Inc.
29 East 21st Street, New York, NY 10010

Library of Congress Cataloging-in-Publication Data

Beutel, Roger.
Writing about issues/Roger Beutel, Lauren Spencer.—1st ed.
    p. cm.—(Write like a pro)
Includes bibliographical references and index.
ISBN 978-1-4488-4682-5 (library binding)—ISBN 978-1-4488-4688-7 (pbk.)—ISBN 978-1-4488-4746-4 (6-pack)
1. Journalism—Authorship—Juvenile literature. 2. Feature writing—Juvenile literature. I. Spencer, Lauren. II. Title.
PN147.B485 2012
808'.06607—dc22

                                                                    2010050038

Manufactured in the United States of America

CPSIA Compliance Information: Batch #S11YA: For further information, contact Rosen Publishing, New York, New York, at 1-800-237-9932.

CONTENTS

INTRODUCTION

I ssue-based writing is a way to keep track and make sense of events going on in the world. It takes a specific subject, whether it's one in the national spotlight or one in the writer's immediate surroundings, and explains that subject so that it can be better understood. By using the five W's—who, what, where, when, and why—along with interview techniques and observations, your issue-based writing piece will convey clear meaning and impact. Journalism, which is writing for media such as newspapers, magazines, and the Internet, uses an issue-based style.

Issue-based stories depend on a writer's own perception of a situation, while providing enough factual information for the reader to understand the facts fully. Issue-based pieces can be written in

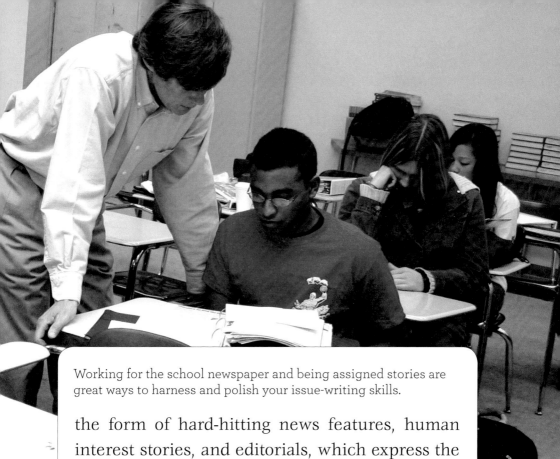

Working for the school newspaper and being assigned stories are great ways to harness and polish your issue-writing skills.

the form of hard-hitting news features, human interest stories, and editorials, which express the writer's opinion.

In this book we will examine how issue-based writing can grow from the beginning of an idea into a solidly researched story. We'll also investigate a variety of writing techniques to understand how issues in our world can come to life in many different ways. Along with the importance of finding an audience for issue-based writing, we will look at ways to capture a reader's attention in just the right manner. The issues don't need to be earth shattering; they just need to move you in such a way that you'll want to know more.

chapter 1

Issue-Writing Techniques and Topic Selection

There are various ways that issue-based pieces can be written. They can be news stories that describe a real event, feature articles that transport the reader into the "shoes" of their subjects, or editorials that express the author's viewpoint. The style in which you choose to write your issue-based piece will depend upon the message and personality you'd like your story to convey.

News Articles

A news article or story takes an event and tells the reader exactly what happened. By focusing on the facts of the story, a

ESSENTIAL STEPS

Understand the various styles used for issue-based writing.

Choose a topic.

Share interesting and timely information with the reader.

news piece delivers a straightforward narrative that sticks to the event being covered without imparting the opinion of its author. Example:

The Windsor Junction town council met last night to consider zoning changes that would allow the proposed sale of Frank Borchardt's 300-acre (121-hectare) farm off of the Stockton Post Road to Pike Brothers, a housing development company. The meeting was open to the public, and the council invited input from interested and concerned town residents.

Pike Brothers has previously stated its intent to build a six hundred-unit housing development on the site if the sale goes through, consisting of three-story houses built according to buyer preference for one of three standard models, with prices starting at $1.2 million. Several councilors indicated that such a development would greatly increase the town's tax base, allowing for increased funding of financially strapped township schools and infrastructure maintenance programs. In addition, the projected eighteen-month building project would generate an estimated one hundred local jobs.

Town residents were less enthusiastic about the proposed sale of the Borchardt farm and the proposed development of the property, though their arguments against the plan varied. Several residents lamented the sale of a farm that was in the Borchardt family since 1753, passed down from one family member to the next over the course of twelve generations. They didn't dispute Frank Borchardt's right to sell the property, but they proposed that the land be bought by the state government instead, as part of its Open Land Initiative.

Other residents didn't oppose the idea of the property's sale and development, but opposed the nature of the Pike Brothers' proposed project. Characterizing it as a gated community for the highly affluent, these residents felt a mixed-income development of single-family houses and apartment buildings for middle- and lower-income residents would be preferable. This would include limited commercial zoning, allowing for the creation of a "village square feel," with a grocery store, drugstore, post office, coffee shop, restaurants, and other family-owned retail businesses. They also proposed a community center that would offer day care, after-school programs, adult education classes, and senior and family programs. Claiming that this kind of integrated village development plan would generate as much tax and other income for the town as would an exclusive housing development, they further argued that it would enhance community spirit and foster stronger relationships among town residents.

It was difficult to tell if any council members were swayed by any of the residents' various arguments and objections. Yet they did decide to delay a vote on the matter in order to take the time to carefully consider the public's feedback and counterproposals.

Feature Stories

A feature story explains an issue from the viewpoint of the main subject. This type of issue-based piece can include more emotional information than a news story because it often relies on the feelings of the subject and author to put the issue in context. Example:

Reading local news is a great way to find ideas for issue-based writing and study examples of how the professionals do it.

At last night's contentious Windsor Junction town council meeting called to decide the fate of a 300-acre (121 ha) farmland property that is the site of a struggle between developers and preservationists, the conflict was nowhere more apparent and dramatic than on the tense and sorrowful face of Frank Borchardt, the man at the center of the controversy.

Borchardt is the owner of the farmland. Indeed, he is the twelfth Borchardt to live and work on the family farm, which was first acquired by his ancestor Eli Borchardt in 1753. Now in his eighties and in failing health, however, Frank no longer has the assistance of his four children, who have all moved to the city for work. Struggling to pay bills and repay various farm loans, Borchardt feels he has no choice but to sell his property to the highest bidder, in this case the McMansion and gated community housing developer Pike Brothers.

Conflicting emotions flickered across Borchardt's face as the meeting progressed and council members and town residents expressed their various and opposing opinions on the proposed property sale: anxiety over his neighbors' and fellow townspeople's anger and disappointment, concern for the meeting's outcome, a certain grim distaste for Pike Brothers' development plans, embarrassment of finding himself in this difficult financial position and having it aired so publicly, and, perhaps most important and poignant, bone-deep sorrow for the imminent loss of his family farm.

At the inconclusive end to the town council meeting, as the debate and arguing spilled outside, no one noticed Borchardt wander out by himself, turn his collar up against the early fall chill, heave himself into his battered old truck, and drive away alone, without a word.

Issue-Based Editorials

An issue-based editorial is focused on the opinion of the writer and is therefore written in the first person. This type of piece reflects clearly how the author feels about a topic. An important point to remember is that an issue-based editorial presents both sides of the issue, while imparting to the reader the reasons why the author feels his or her opinion is worthwhile. Example:

Though there was scarce consensus at last night's Windsor Junction town council meeting regarding future plans for Frank Borchardt's farmland, there was one point that nearly all in attendance agreed upon: it was a genuine shame for both Mr. Borchardt and the town that he and his family can no longer afford to keep their farm in operation.

Mr. Borchardt's sons and daughters all felt compelled to move to the city to find work and earn a decent wage. The economics of small-scale farming just don't work in their favor, and there were neither enough job opportunities or affordable housing in town to keep them close to the farm and able to pitch in together to keep it running.

This hard and sad reality is a reflection of a larger problem for Windsor Junction. Over 70 percent of our children feel compelled to go outside the area for their higher education and for employment. They rarely, if ever, return. Their common complaint is that there are no jobs that pay and no housing that they can afford. The result is an aging population, a stagnating local economy, a diminishing tax base, and a community lacking in youth, vibrancy, and multigenerational family ties.

Time marches on; the world changes and evolves. We all know and acknowledge this. Windsor Junction is not going to regain the tens of thousands of acres of farm and woodland it has lost to development. Frank Borchardt's 300 acres (121 ha) are as good as sold. That farm, too, won't be coming back. But its loss can be transformed into a rare gain for the town. In order to make this happy outcome come about, the town council should reject Pike Brothers' plan for an elitist enclave of million-dollar mansions and instead approve the Citizen Committee's counterproposal for a mixed-income, mixed-use, village-within-a-village development. The affordable houses and apartments of this residential and commercial development will attract and retain young people and families, as will the shops and community services. A vibrant, lively, economically viable and active community will emerge, revitalizing all of Windsor Junction, calling our children and grandchildren back home. It will also serve as a worthy tribute to the founding Borchardt family and the hundreds of years of passion, labor, tears, and love they put into this cherished plot of land.

Choosing a Topic

Now that you've decided on an issue-based style, you need a topic to write about. There are interesting topics all around you. Issue-based topics need to deal with a situation of interest to both you and your readers. Think of a subject that is timely and gripping. You may have already been assigned a topic to cover for an issue-based piece, but if not, look around you for

Rewriting the News

Look at the newspaper, watch the news, or go to an online news source and find a story. Examine it and then rewrite the story using each of these issue-based techniques:

- As a news story using just the facts
- As a feature story through the eyes of the main character
- As an opinion piece expressing how you feel about the story

ideas, or read the community section of your local newspaper. Make a note when something catches your eye or ear. Ask yourself questions as you look around you. Is something happening in your community that may affect others? If so, how will it affect them and why?

A sure way to invite your readers to climb inside your issue-based story is to find something that they will feel strongly about. Look at what is happening in your neighborhood. People love to relate to a situation in which they know the location and the people involved.

Issues that tug at the heart or involve drama or conflict make great topics for issue-based stories. Keep in mind that a certain amount of time may go by between when you decide on a topic and when you write the story, so make sure that the issue you cover is one that has "legs." This term that reporters sometimes use means a story has enough meaning to stand the test of time.

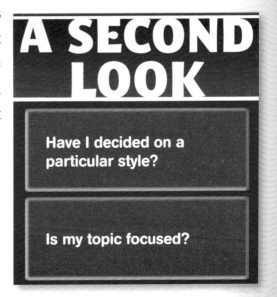

A SECOND LOOK

Have I decided on a particular style?

Is my topic focused?

chapter 2
Information Gathering

With an issue-based topic, the investigation and research you do before you start writing your first draft is very important. It is the gathering of information that will fill out your news story, feature, or editorial so that the reader will feel that he or she is getting the full picture.

There are many different resources available to help you gather the information you need. First of all, a curious mind is necessary. Take your topic and do some investigating. If you are writing about something you've heard, make a list of people you can talk to who will have information about this issue. Interviewing is a great way to get first-hand facts about your subject. Before you approach the people you want to interview, come

ESSENTIAL STEPS

Understand how to use your time and resources in order to meet your deadline.

Research your topic.

Focus your point of view.

up with questions to ask them. Be prepared with a series of important points that you want to go over so that you get as much out of the moment as you can. Be relaxed and focused so that the interview will be more like a conversation, rather than an interrogation.

Finding Your Angle

As you speak with people, be open to the fact that your idea may shift a little as you investigate it further. For instance, if you are pursuing a story on your school's sudden decision to cut its baseball program to save money, you may find out by talking to people that interest and participation in baseball has been waning steadily for years. At the same time, newer athletic offerings like lacrosse, golf, and soccer have been increasing in popularity. Changing athletic trends and preferences may prove to be a more interesting direction for the article to take, so a slight shift in your focus would make the story better.

As you dive deeper into the topic, consider your angle. The angle of the story is the point of view that you, the author, bring to the piece. It is the foundation on which the story is built. Developing a solid angle will help keep you on track as you gather information.

Turning an interview into a naturally flowing, wide-ranging conversation is a great way to get valuable information from a source and an important skill to develop.

A good way to keep your viewpoint focused and your information organized is with a graphic organizer called a gathering grid. This method of organizing is often combined with notes taken on index cards. This will help you keep track of your thoughts and your sources. Sources, which are places where you find information, can include books, magazines and other periodicals, the Internet, and people you interviewed for the story.

Using a Gathering Grid

At the top of a blank computer spreadsheet or sheet of paper, identify your topic. Down the left-hand side of the spreadsheet, compose a list of questions using the basic five W's (who, what, where, when, why) in no particular order. In the columns, input the source where the information was found. Then, on the index cards, write what that information is. Color-code your index cards for easy access.

TOPIC: Changing Trends in High School Sports

	Interviews (blue index cards)	Newspaper (yellow index cards)	Magazine (green index cards)	Internet (white index cards)
What sports are attracting students who used to play baseball?	Coach Vernor, athletic director (note 1)		*Sports Illustrated* on the waning of interest in baseball at the high school level (note 6)	
How will the dismantling of the baseball team affect the school athletic budget?	Ms. Springer, school board member (note 2)	Article in local paper about school finances and budget cutting measures (note 7)		School district's Web site (note 4)
Who is making the decision about what sports are offered at the school?	Coach Vernor (note 1); Coach Cudahee, baseball coach (note 4)			
Why is interest in baseball beginning to wane?		School newspaper article on baseball team's difficulty in fielding enough players (note 5)	*Sporting News* article on growing popularity of lacrosse and soccer at high school level (note 6)	
What will happen to the baseball fields? Will they be converted to lacrosse and soccer fields?	Coach Vernor (note 1); Tom Pruitt, school groundskeeper (note 4)			School Planning Commission Web site (note 4)
When will the school's baseball team play its last game?	Coach Vernor (note 8); Coach Cudahee (note 9)	Local newspaper feature article on school's last baseball team and its last game (note 12)	Article on the history of the school's baseball program in alumni magazine (note 11)	
Where will students still interested in baseball be able to play at the high school level?	Coach Vernor (note 8); Coach Cudahee (note 9); Jim Doyle, president of the county's Babe Ruth Baseball League (note 13)			Babe Ruth Baseball League Web site (note 13)

Example (blue index card for Interviews):

Note 9, Coach Cudahee: "That last game on May 17 is going to be a tough one for all of us. There's just so much history and great memories and generations of players we're sort of packing away and saying good-bye to. It's such a shame, a real end of an era. But we'll have to find a way to master our emotions, focus on the game at hand, and find a way to pull out one more victory. One last victory, I guess."

STRATEGIES FOR A SUCCESSFUL INTERVIEW

- Find the right person for the topic—make sure that he or she is informed.
- Set up the interview by allowing enough time to talk without feeling rushed.
- Do not ask questions that only require a "yes" or "no" answer. Ask the question in such a way that the subject has to give an explanation. By starting your question with "how" (or, "who," "what," "when," "where," or "why"), you will be guaranteed a more detailed answer.
- Have your questions written in the order you'd like them answered, but be flexible enough to allow more free-form follow-up questions.
- Listen carefully. This will lead to follow-up questions because the person might say something that will lead to another interesting point.

Selecting Sources

The Internet and library are useful for gathering information for your grid. These resources offer a chance to look through articles in books, magazines, or newspapers. You can use a search engine and go to Web sites for research, too. To search, enter your topic, for example, "high school baseball program eliminated," and examine a wide variety of articles about the same issue.

Be very sure of the facts that you gather from all of your sources. If you are unsure about something, ask someone who can either confirm or deny the statement. Not everything we read online or in print is factual, so have a healthy amount of skepticism. This way you'll be sure that the story you write is not only factually correct but also offers a balanced point of view.

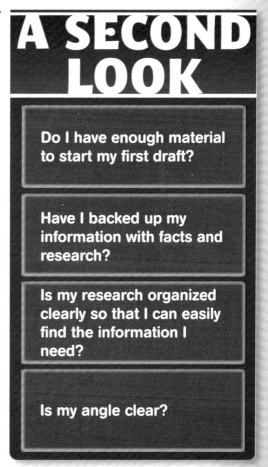

A SECOND LOOK

Do I have enough material to start my first draft?

Have I backed up my information with facts and research?

Is my research organized clearly so that I can easily find the information I need?

Is my angle clear?

chapter 3
The First Draft

The details you have gathered will now become the material for your issue-based piece. Before you begin writing the story, make sure you have its nuts and bolts clear in your head. These are the five W's around which issue-based pieces revolve.

To clarify your vision and reestablish your angle or point of view, make a list of the basic five W's in your story. Whether you are writing a news piece, feature article, or an editorial, you will need these basic, concrete facts before you begin. Use this information to form your paragraphs while incorporating the details and quotes you've gathered during your research.

ESSENTIAL STEPS

Organize the details.

Begin writing.

Use facts, anecdotes, and quotes.

The beginning of the piece contains its vital information. The story information then unfolds into supporting facts and anecdotes, which are brief stories that illustrate the topic or prove a point. In

Example:
Topic: Group of students protest locker searches by walking out of afternoon classes

Who?: Allison Barr, John Wentzel, Erin Hutchinson, Maureen Edinfield

What?: Suspended after cutting afternoon classes

When?: Last week

Where?: Windsor Junction Junior High School

Why?: Students walked out of class in protest of local police search of all students' lockers

order to bring your reader into the heart of your story, you'll want to develop a lead sentence that creates interest in the story by immediately grabbing the reader's attention. Take your time developing your lead sentence by looking over your notes for something that stands out. Example:

They did it in silence and in complete solidarity. As if summoned by a bell unheard by anyone else, the four students rose simultaneously, calmly gathered their things, and left the classroom silently, without making any angry speeches or even offering a word of explanation. Their quiet resolve and dignified determination spoke volumes on their behalf.

By using something that puts the reader immediately into the moment, you've made him or her want to continue reading. From here, lay out the details and use your facts and anecdotes, along with quoted material, to bring the story to life. Each paragraph should add more information to support the subject. In your last paragraph, summarize and restate key points.

As you write your first draft, have all of the research you've gathered within reach or easily accessible. Your first draft is an opportunity to write all of your ideas without interruption. Do not worry about using correct spelling or grammar because those corrections will come during the editing of your piece. Even if you find places where you feel you need more information, don't let it stop you; just make a note and keep writing. You can go back to add more data later. Example:

They did it in silence and in complete solidarity. As if summoned by a bell unheard by anyone else, the four students rose simultaneously, calmly gathered their things, and left the classroom silently, without making any angry speeches or even offering a word of explanation. Their quiet resolve and dignified determination spoke volumes on their behalf.

Nevertheless, school administrators sought and received an explanation from the four students—Allison Barr, John Wentzel, Erin Hutchinson, and Maureen Edinfield. Notified by their seventh-period social studies teacher, Stewart Cunningham, that the students had inexplicably left his room just minutes after the class began, Assistant Principal Stanley Green found the four loitering in the school parking lot. After ushering them into his office, he asked Principal Joanna Bertucci to join them.

Any good issue-based piece of writing will require thorough research and scrupulous fact-checking.

Green demanded to know what their reason for leaving class was. According to accounts provided by both Assistant Principal Green and John Wentzel, Erin Hutchinson served as the group spokesperson. She stated that the four students, outraged by the recent search of all student lockers by local police officers, had decided to protest by walking out of class. "The police had neither probable cause nor a search warrant. That makes this an illegal search according to the Fourth and Fourteenth Amendments to the U.S. Constitution. Our constitutional rights were violated," Hutchinson declared. "And, incidentally, no drugs or weapons were found."

If Principals Green and Bertucci were impressed by the political convictions and constitutional knowledge of these four students, their sense of duty to school rules overrode any inclination to be lenient. Principal Bertucci calmly but firmly replied to Hutchinson's declaration by stating that it was school policy to invite local police into the school for unannounced locker searches as much as four times a year and that this complied with state search-and-seizure guidelines governing public schools. She further reminded the four students that absence from class without permission or a valid excuse was grounds for detention and possible suspension. Hutchinson, Wentzel, Edinfield, and Barr were given a week's worth of detentions and threatened with suspension for a second offense.

However, their social studies teacher, Mr. Cunningham, couldn't help but admire his students' moxie. "I should be offended that they walked out on my class," he said. "But they obviously have been listening to what I've been teaching, and they acted in a manner consistent with the constitutional principles and precedents we've been studying and discussing in class. They provided the whole school with a living civics lesson. I'm tempted to give them extra credit!"

For their part, the students feel satisfied that they made their point and are willing to take their punishment stoically. "Do the crime, serve the time," quipped Barr. Yet another civics lesson provided by Windsor Junction Junior High's "Gang of Four."

This news piece used all of the five W's within the early paragraphs. If needed, the piece could be cut from the bottom because all of the essential facts of this particular story were covered in the first four paragraphs. The author also did research to find out the school's policy on both police searches and unexcused absence from class, supplied quotes to illustrate and support that research, and related anecdotes about the actual events surrounding the student protest. Quoted material was used to support the general topic.

Remember, any time you use a person's words, whether written in a book, taken from a Web site, or from an interview, you must put them in quotation marks. If you write those words as if they were your own, then you are plagiarizing someone else's work. Plagiarism is very serious. In order to avoid this, make sure that you keep track of where you've gotten your information. This way you can give proper credit to the author or interviewee.

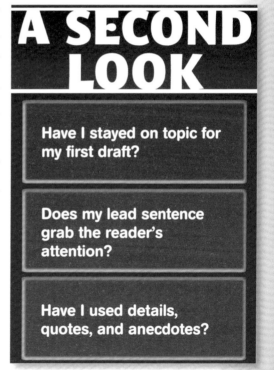

A SECOND LOOK

Have I stayed on topic for my first draft?

Does my lead sentence grab the reader's attention?

Have I used details, quotes, and anecdotes?

chapter 4
Revising What You Have Written

After you've finished the first draft of your issue-based piece, think about a title that will enhance your article. A title is very important for issue-based writing because it is the first thing to grab a reader's attention. Even before your lead sentence draws a reader in, a title will make someone want to know more. Think about a title that is concise and to the point. Focus on active verbs to get your view across. Don't use the same wording as your lead sentence.

For a news article, see how you can summarize the event without being obvious. For instance, if your piece is about the fact that the school library does not have enough high-caliber and high-speed digital resources, come up with something more appealing than "Library's Resources Are Outdated."

ESSENTIAL STEPS

Add a catchy or playful title.

Revisit the piece to determine if more research is needed.

Clarify sentences, paragraphs, and transitions.

Think about something specific to tie in the theme, like "School Library Idles on the Shoulder of the Digital Superhighway." Wordplay on the subject can elicit a reader's attention and pique his or her curiosity.

Editorial pieces depend on your viewpoint to transport the reader into the writing; therefore, a title expressing your opinion is in order. Think about how you might announce your point of view out loud. Something like "Windsor Junction High's School Library Is Stuck in the Stone Age" will give the reader direct insight into your feelings. With all issue-based titles, you want to leave just enough to the imagination so that the reader is curious enough to read on.

Going Back with Fresh Eyes

Revision gives you the chance to look again at what you've written and make it even better. It's a sign that you think highly of your work and want to improve it. For the most productive view of what you've written, take a break from your story and let it "breathe." This will allow you to get a fresh perspective on the writing, as if you're seeing it again for the first time. Don't wait too long to get back to it, though. You don't want to lose interest and then let the piece go unfinished, since your excitement about the subject is what makes it fresh.

It's a good idea to study the work of writers you admire to get a feel for how they use language, sentence construction, and rhythm to achieve their masterly effects.

Once you pick it up again, use a colored pen or pencil, and read the piece aloud. You can do this just for yourself or in front of someone else. Mark any words that you stumble over or sentences that are confusing. Then you can come back and make changes.

Note the additions or edits clearly on your page. Make sure that the meaning of your piece is as clear as possible. If you find that your sentences are too long, look for where they can be simplified and broken up into more concise thoughts. Also make sure that each paragraph contains just one main idea. As one thought comes to an end and another begins, start a new paragraph.

Choosing Sentences for Greatest impact

Sentences are meant to deliver all kinds of messages, so the way you write them will add to their impact. There are choices in the types of sentences you can use to get your point across in an interesting way.

THE BUILDING BLOCKS OF GOOD WRITING

All writers must adhere to some basic rules if they want to sharpen their writing skills.

Concept: The main idea or topic of your written work is like a tree trunk. Its main points are like branches that flow from the concept's base. Informative details can grow like budding leaves from those branches and can take the form of detailed descriptions, anecdotes, quoted or para-phrased information, statistics, and other hard data.

Order: The way in which your tree—or concept—grows, or the way it is organized, is as important as your main idea. While there are many ways to orga-nize your piece, you must adhere to whatever design you have chosen. Having a good organiza-tional structure in place will help you make the transitions from point to point more easily.

Style: The style of a written work is sometimes referred to as the "author's voice." Your author's voice is like a personal signature that only you can give your work.

Word Choice: Using precise words to convey specific meanings or emotion in your work is as important as your concept, order, and author's voice. Always review your draft to make sure that each word that you have chosen is the best word to express the full and exact meaning of your concept or idea.

Rhythm: The flow of sentences in your writing determines if the work has rhythm and momentum. As a rule, you want to vary the sentence length and structure throughout your written work. Always read your work aloud to get a sense of its overall rhythm.

Mechanics: The mechanical elements of your writing are the key points that determine if it is correct or not. These elements include the conventions of spelling, grammar, usage, punctuation, capitalization, and creat-

Sentences That Are Simple

A simple sentence states a single complete thought using a subject and predicate. Example:

The library's computers are old and slow.
(subject)   (predicate)

Sentences That Are Compound

A compound sentence joins two or more simple sentences, either with punctuation or a coordinating conjunction. Coordinating conjunctions are joining words such as "and," "or," "but," and "so". Examples:

The library's computers are old and slow; it's very frustrating.

(A semicolon is used to join these two complete sentences.)

The library's computers are old and slow, so it's very frustrating.

(A coordinating conjunction is used to join the two complete sentences.)

Sentences That Are Complex

When a sentence contains a dependent clause, which can't stand alone because it's an incomplete thought, it's called a complex sentence. Example:

The library's digital database, which is very small and outdated, makes me frustrated.

(The dependent clause "which is very small and outdated" adds more detail.)

Sentences That Are Declarative

This type of sentence makes a statement. Example:

The school library's digital resources are inadequate for students' needs.

Sentences That Are Interrogative

An interrogative sentence is a question. Example:

When should a library computer be considered too old for student use and be replaced?

Asking Rhetorical Questions

A rhetorical question is a question for which no response is expected. Example:

Don't students deserve the best digital technology available to them?

Sentences That Are Imperative

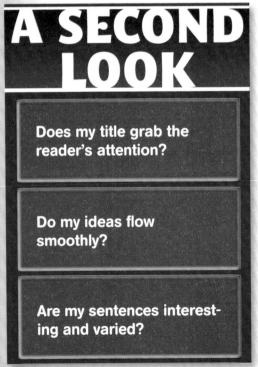

A SECOND LOOK

Does my title grab the reader's attention?

Do my ideas flow smoothly?

Are my sentences interesting and varied?

An imperative sentence gives a command to the reader. Example:

Consider how different the research process would be for students if the school library invested in new technology.

Sentences That Are Exclamatory

An exclamatory sentence relays a strong sense of emotion. Example:

Proofreading Marks

∧	Insert letters, words, or sentences
ℐ	Delete
⌃	Insert a comma
⌄	Apostrophe or single quotation mark
⌄⌄	Double quotation marks
∿	Transpose elements (switch the order)
#	Insert a space
⊃	Close up this space
⊙	Use a period here
¶	Begin new paragraph
no¶	No paragraph

Having access to cutting-edge, high-tech, twenty-first century library resources would be enormously helpful and reason to cheer!

If you use a variety of sentence styles, your reader will get the most that he or she can out of your story. Take time to examine all the sentences in your draft to determine if they should be more varied.

chapter 5

Editing What You Have Written

Before your issue-based story makes an appearance in the world, you'll want to make sure that the facts you've used are correct. In order to fact-check a story, you'll need to have your research and interviews handy for reference. Go over the proper names you've used to make sure they are spelled correctly. Make sure that every person's job title is correct. If you have any questions about these issues, double-check them in order to verify the information. Often, if the person works in an office, there will be someone there that can help you.

ESSENTIAL STEPS

Make sure facts and names are correct.

Ask someone else to read your draft and check for errors.

Complete a spelling and grammar check.

Any dates, whether they are of births, deaths, or national or local events, need to be checked for accuracy. Encyclopedias are a great source for general information, while a local city office will often have data to confirm events or dates in your immediate area. The Internet is also a great resource for fact-checking, since you can usually find respected encyclopedias, government information, and other reputable material online.

Take your time when you are fact-checking your issue-based piece. Never be embarrassed to re-approach a person you've interviewed to make sure you've gotten his or her quotes and information correct. This shows respect for the person you interviewed as well as for your readers.

Seeking the Help of Critical Readers

Once all your thoughts and facts are in order, enlist outside help. This step will be very important in giving you confidence to stand behind your work with pride. Choose someone who you know will spend time reading your article and who you can trust to give you an honest opinion of it. Friends or family members can be of help as long as you let them know that you need them to share their thoughts honestly and constructively. Often people who are close to us feel that they might hurt our feelings with criticism, but constructive criticism is always useful. This is when someone comments on exactly how to make something better

Be sure to refer to dictionaries and grammar guides when proofreading and revising your work.

as opposed to just saying "It's OK" or "It doesn't sound right."

You can also choose to use constructive criticism in a group setting by reading your issue-based article aloud to several people. Have a question-and-answer session afterward. This is helpful to find out which part of the piece people responded to the most or were confused by. This might give you ideas for moving certain ideas closer to the beginning or dropping certain facts altogether.

A Final Proofread

Once you've made all your changes, it's time to do a final spelling and grammar check. If you're working with a hard copy, use a colored pen to circle any questionable words and look them up in the dictionary. If your piece was written using a computer, employ the spell-check function. Your computer will also probably have a grammar-check function. But if it doesn't, or if your piece is handwritten, check your punctuation and grammar with a reference manual. Example:

Document1

A Cyberplague Sweeping Through Our School

There's a new menace stalking our school hallways, threatening the physical, mental, and emotional lives of students. In some cases, it even kills. It's not some new and dangerous drug or a previously unknown deadly virus. It's not an ultra-caffeinated, highly alcoholic beverage or a high-fat, high-calorie, sweet and salty junk food. Rather, it is a high-tech variant on an age-old problem: bullying. Twenty-first century tools and technology have transformed bullying into cyberbullying, and this form of aggression and violence is far from virtual. It is very real, and it happens in our school every day.

The Cyberbullying Research Center defines cyberbullying as the harassment, mistreatment, or mockery of another person online or while using cell phones or other electronic devices. In February 2010, it released the results of a survey it conducted among 4,441 young people between the ages of 10 and 18. The survey found that 20 percent of these students had experienced cyberbullying in their lifetimes, Almost 14 percent of the respondents had been the victim of mean or hurtful online comments in the past thirty days, while almost 13 percent had been the victim of malicious rumors spread online in the past month. Seventeen percent of the survey respondents had been cyberbullied two or more times in the past thirty days. And anecdotal evidence exists that clearly indicates

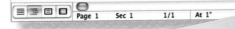

Page 1   Sec 1   1/1   At 1"   TRK EXT OVR

that Windsor Junction High is not only not immune from this scourge, but actually seriously afflicted by it.

A ninth-grade girl, who wishes to remain anonymous, told me recently that for the past six months she had received daily e-mails from a group of well-known, popular girls calling her names, criticizing her appearance, and saying everyone hates her. They have also spread rumors and disparaging comments about her via Twitter and Facebook. Their boyfriends have posted photos of her that have been doctored to embarrass and humiliate her. She says all of this harassment has her considering switching schools. She admits that she has even considered suicide. And her story is not an isolated one or even the most dramatic. Scores of students have come to me in private when they heard I was writing an editorial for the school paper about cyberbullying in the hopes that it would somehow make a difference, perhaps by providing a wake-up call for teachers, administrators, and parents.

When confronted with these stories of cyberbullying, Principal Bertucci argued that the situation was more complex than it appeared and the administration had to tread carefully when sorting through accusations of misbehavior. She stated that she personally investigates every alleged act of cyberbullying brought to her attention, though she suspects that only about one in four victims actually reports the harassment to teachers or administrators.

Bertucci pointed out that, unfortunately, evidence for these crimes is not always as plentiful or straightforward as might be expected. For example, several accused bullies have claimed that someone used their e-mail account or cell phone without permission to send bullying messages. In such cases, without additional evidence, the principal has no choice but to take the suspect at his or her word. The privacy rights of students prevent Bertucci from seizing and searching cell phones, e-mail accounts, and personal laptop computers. Any attempts to seek and receive parental permission to search accused students' accounts and devices have been met with refusal and threats of lawsuit.

Without hard and fast proof or parental support, Bertucci laments, there is little she can do other than issue stern warnings and carefully monitor on-site student computer and digital activity. "My heart aches for these kids," Bertucci said. "I so badly want to help and protect them, and I am doing that to the best of my ability. But in many ways, my hands are tied. I really need parents to get on board with anti-bullying measures that will give me some real tools to fix what's wrong here."

Given the amount of suffering I have witnessed and been privy to among my fellow students, and considering the recent spate of suicides among cyberbullied teens, I feel school administrators, teachers, parents, and students alike must join together and confront this digital menace and the cowards who hide safely behind their computer screens. We all must come together and strip these cyberbullies of their weapons, even if that means sacrificing some of our own rights.

Cell phones should be banned from school grounds and confiscated if found or if suspected in a case of cyberbullying. Personal laptop computers should also be banned in school. All computer use should only occur in a supervised computer lab. All activity on those computers should be stored on the server for retrieval during investigations of cyberbullying. Certain sites like social networking Web sites or personal e-mail accounts should be blocked. E-mail and instant messaging should only be sent via school accounts. If anyone's e-mail account is linked to a cyberbullying incident, that person should be held accountable and punished, even if he or she claims the account was used by someone else without permission. Finally, penalties for cyberbullying should be increased and strengthened, beginning with suspension, peer mediation, and mandatory sensitivity training. Cyberbullying guidelines and penalties should be clearly spelled out in the student handbook distributed to students and their parents, removing any legal impediment to effective punishment and prevention measures.

It is only by taking a hard line and adopting a zero-tolerance policy on cyberbullying that we will effectively enforce minimum standards of civility on campus and make school safe for all students, not just for those with the loudest and ugliest voices.

This editorial piece grabs the reader's attention with its title. It also uses all the five W's in the first two paragraphs. The author did research and interviewed a source for the piece. All of those items and quotes were fact-checked for accuracy. Notice that the source of the cyberbullying statistics was included and that Principal Bertucci's statement was put in quotation marks. Also, note how the editorial writer's conclusion is clearly summarized in the article's final statement.

A SECOND LOOK

Have I checked all name spellings, quotes, and facts for accuracy?

Are constructive criticisms incorporated?

Is the final spelling and grammar check complete?

chapter 6

Go Digital! Presenting Your Writing

As you put your issue-based piece into its final form, think about how quickly most people respond to what something looks like. The presentation of your piece will make an important first impression on your reader. No matter what style of issue-based writing you have chosen, your final draft should be straightforward in font style and size. Whether your story is handwritten or composed on a computer, it needs to be clear and legible so that your audience is not distracted from its content. Finally, check that your name appears clearly on your article.

Publishing and Posting Your Work

ESSENTIAL STEPS

Investigate different visual elements.

Find opportunities to present and share your work.

You can share your issue-based piece in a variety of ways. If your school has a newspaper or magazine, approach its staff with your story. You can also volunteer for assignments through a school newspaper or magazine if you decide you'd like to be further involved in the world of journalism. Think about a local community paper or magazine that might publish your take on an issue-based story. These types of publications usually focus on local events, so if your issue-based piece fits that category, send it in. Remember always to check the submission guidelines first.

There are also opportunities for publishing your piece in age-appropriate national magazines. Online, you can find a list of publications to which you can send your work. Always check with an adult before submitting stories online because it's important to have another set of eyes look over any rules and regulations that may apply. Also, an adult can make sure that the site is reputable and safe. Online publications often have very specific submission requirements. Follow them closely, so that your writing ends up in the right hands.

A new trend in issue-based reporting has emerged, driven by the Internet, digital cameras and video, and texting and tweeting. It is known as "citizen journalism," and many mainstream news organizations now welcome breaking news submissions from ordinary people.

One such web site is CNN iReport, affiliated with the CNN cable news network and Web site. CNN invites ordinary people to report on newsworthy events that they witness or investigate. It also allows them to share their opinion pieces. These can be posted to the iReport Web site and viewed by the entire world. Some of the most compelling, important, and urgent of these reported stories and opinion pieces are chosen by CNN producers, carefully reviewed and cleared for use, and become part of CNN's broadcast and Web news coverage.

Unless a piece is chosen by a producer for use by CNN, an iReport piece will not be edited, fact-checked, or screened by CNN before it is posted. So it is up to the author to get all the facts correct and make the writing as clear, grammatical, and compelling as possible. If the author does not take the time to get all of the details right, there is little chance that the post will be picked up by CNN for broadcast. Lots of local newspapers are also encouraging their readers to contribute news stories, photos, and video of any breaking news they witness.

Another venue for posting and sharing one's issue-based writing, particularly opinion pieces, is the Web site Daily Kos (http://www.dailykos.com). This political and issue-driven Web site bills itself as an online political community, news organization, and activist

A billboard advertises CNN's online and international "citizen journalism" site, one of many such sites that have appeared on the Internet.

hub. It features articles written by permanent staff members, as well as guest pieces written by prominent politicians. Yet through the Daily Kos Diaries section, any visitor may post their writing. They can even create their own Web page within Daily Kos that features their archive of "diary entries." If a particular entry gets a lot of favorable feedback from readers or catches the eye of a staffer, it may be selected by the site's editors for prominent placement on the site's home page.

One very easy and instantaneous way to post and share your writing and opinions is to write thoughtful and respectful responses to online articles that you read. Most online articles conclude with a comments section that users can enter to provide feedback on what they've just read. It's sort of an instant "Letters to the Editor" feature—instantly received and instantly published. Your feedback may generate a debate among several other readers, stimulating a lively discussion. The article's author may join in or respond to your comments. Your writing may even draw the attention of the site's editors.

You should also consider designing your own blog, perhaps centering upon local issues: news, politics, town government, current events, goings-on about town, entertainment, or community involvement/activism. This would provide you with the perfect venue for ongoing writing projects that involve news reporting and investigation, news analysis, feature stories, human interest stories, and opinion pieces. It may attract the attention of local newspaper editors and town leaders, opening up new writing and professional opportunities for you. Your blog may even become the must-read Web site in your town. You may become an important clearinghouse for information, an influential tastemaker and opinion-maker, and a major player in local events.

Observe Proper Netiquette

The Internet has made it easy to post and share one's work with a wide audience and receive immediate feedback. This is an exciting and exhilarating development. Yet it also comes with some drawbacks and dangers.

You must be prepared for criticism, some of it fair and constructive, some harsh, and some just plain mean and abusive. If you receive a harsh or abusive comment or review, do not respond in kind. Things can escalate and get out of control very quickly, and you may become banned from the site. It's best not to respond, or, if you feel you must, respond with great politeness and civility, saying that you are essentially agreeing to disagree. If you feel the person who has left a comment has crossed the line of decency, report that person to the site's webmaster. Do not get drawn into a war of words. Do not stoop to their level. And never write a comment about someone else's work that you would not want to receive yourself.

Engaging an abusive critic online can quickly open the door to harassment, cyberbullying, and flaming. Cyberbullying is the use of digital technologies to express deliberate, repeated, and hostile behaviors toward others. It can happen through e-mail, text messages, instant messages, blogs, or chat rooms in a private or a public format. Social networking sites such as Facebook, Twitter, and MySpace have become places where bullying occasionally occurs among students and other young people. Even minor cases of cyberbullying can affect a person's well-being, making it difficult to go online, concentrate, or even study or do homework. Severe instances of cyberbullying have led to criminal attacks. In several cases, it has even led to the suicide of the bullying victim.

The best way to stop the problem is to address it directly and do something about it. Report the cyberbully to the webmaster and do not continue to talk to the bully, neither in person (if you know him or her) nor via electronic communication. It is important to involve a trusted adult in the problem.

The word "flaming" refers to the hostile or insulting interactions that people can have on the Internet. People tend to say things on the Internet that they wouldn't feel comfortable saying in person. People tend to feel more comfortable expressing anger, disgust, or disapproval in written form over the Internet. Leaving comments on someone's blog post, Facebook, MySpace, or Twitter page that are rude or insulting is not good "netiquette."

People often engage in flaming on blogs, chat rooms, message boards, or other sites where people are invited to post reviews of someone's writings or of consumer products, music, movies, or books. Strangers can get into arguments in these dis-cussion threads, with an unlimited number of people able to view their comments. Sometimes, once one aggressive user attacks someone who has posted a comment he or she disagrees with, other users feel emboldened to join in and gang up on the flaming victim. Flamers turn what should be supportive and stimu-lating environments into

The Golden Rule of Netiquette is, when online, treat others as you wish to be treated.

ones poisoned by anger, dread, intimidation, fear, and, ultimately, silence.

Just as you do not want your writing to be savaged and do not want to be the victim of flaming, you must never attack someone online. Do not hide behind the idea that what you are posting is anonymous because people do not know you or your real name. Think about what you are posting. Would you be willing to deliver this message to the person face-to-face? Think about whether the statement you are posting is something you would like to read about yourself. Just think of what it would be like for all of your friends, family, classmates, and acquaintances to read unflattering things about you on your personal page or in the comments section of a posting.

Be cautious, too, about any images or videos you post to your blog or use as accompaniment to a posted article. Avoid posting overly personal, private, or inappropriate content on your blog, Web site, or social networking site. Not only do you have limited control (at best) over who can view this material, it will also continue to exist on the Web long after you post it—and probably long after you come to regret it.

Copyright

Copyright is a form of intellectual property law that protects original creative works. This includes literary, dramatic, musical, and artistic material, such as poetry, novels, movies, songs, computer software, and architecture. Copyright covers both published and unpublished works.

Current copyright law protects any work you create that is tangible and can be viewed or read either directly or with the aid of a machine or device. You do not have to register for a copyright to receive copyright protection; it is conferred automatically at the work's creation. Yet many people wish to register for a copyright in order to obtain a public record of the copyright and to enable them to sue anyone who uses their work without permission.

You should be aware that when you post your writing to a Web site, in most cases you are surrendering your copyright to that site. The Web site retains the right to use your material as it sees fit without your further permission. It can even publish and distribute your material without your agreement and without reimbursement.

In addition, it is your responsibility to ensure that you have not violated anyone else's copyright in your posted work, by, for example, plagiarizing or pasting in large chunks of someone else's text without permission. Most Web sites that post users' writing do not provide fact-checking services. They also do not seek legal permission for the use of any other person's material that you may be quoting or pasting into your work. These tasks are all your responsibility. You should always read the Web site's terms of use, user agreement, submission guidelines, and Web site policies pages before posting your work. This will help you determine if you are surrendering your copyright, what the site may do with your work, and if you have met all your obligations regarding your work's accuracy, quality, completeness, and avoidance of copyright infringement. You must also follow the site's rules about proper etiquette while using the site and its guidelines concerning proper and improper content.

If you wish to post and share your work but retain the copyright, consider creating your own blog that you can control. Even on your own blog, however, you must not violate someone else's copyright by using their material—photos, video clips, extended quotes—without permission.

Digging Deeper, Sharpening Skills

If journalism interests you, try taking classes offered at your school or at the local community college. Try working as a writer or editor for your school newspaper. You can also read books or Web sites related to issue-based writing to sharpen your skills. But the main thing is to just start writing about anything that matters to you, every day!

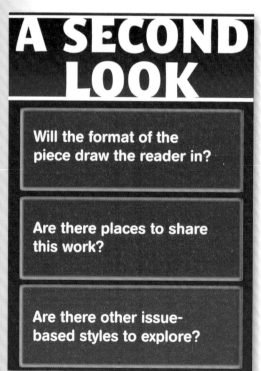

A SECOND LOOK

Will the format of the piece draw the reader in?

Are there places to share this work?

Are there other issue-based styles to explore?

GLOSSARY

anecdote A short, entertaining account of an event.

angle The viewpoint of the piece.

article A complete piece of writing, as in a newspaper or magazine.

assignment A task or mission.

chronological In the order that events happened.

complex sentence A sentence formed by one independent clause and one or more dependent clauses.

compound sentence A sentence in which two independent clauses are joined together with a coordinate conjunction.

conjunction A word used to connect individual words or groups of words.

constructive criticism Helpful remarks about someone's writing.

content The substance of a piece; what is contained in a body of writing.

deadline The date or time by which something has to be completed.

declarative sentence A sentence that makes a strong statement.

dependent clause A clause that cannot stand on its own and depends on the rest of the sentence to make sense.

essay A piece of writing where a single topic is presented, explained, and described in an interesting way.

first draft The first writing of a piece without worrying about mistakes.

format The style or manner of a piece of writing.

heading Words located at the top of the page that include pertinent information about time, place, and author.

imperative sentence A sentence that gives a command to the reader.

independent clause A statement that expresses a complete thought and can stand alone as a sentence.

interrogative sentence A sentence in the form of a question.

journalism The collecting and editing of news for presentation through the media.

nonfiction Stories that are true.

paragraph A passage of writing of one or more sentences that deals with a single topic.

phrase A group of related words that do not express complete thoughts or form a complete sentence.

plagiarism The taking of ideas or writing from an author and passing them off as one's own.

proofreading Checking the final copy for any errors.

reporter A person who gathers and reports news.

revise To go back and survey with an eye to making changes or corrections.

rhetorical question A question for which no response or answer is expected.

source A person or place where information comes from.

subject The topic of a writing piece.

title The heading of a piece of writing.

topic The subject of a written work.

transition A word or phrase that smoothly ties two ideas together.

verb A word that describes or indicates action.

FOR MORE INFORMATION

Alliance for Young Artists & Writers

557 Broadway

New York, NY 10012

Web site: http://www.artandwriting.org

The Alliance for Young Artists & Writers, a nonprofit organization, identifies teenagers with exceptional artistic and literary talent and brings their work to a national audience through the Scholastic Art & Writing Awards.

***Amazing Kids!* Magazine**

20126 Ballinger Way NE, Suite 239

Shoreline, WA 98155

(206) 331-3807

Web site: http://www.amazing-kids.org

This is a kid-created online magazine and Web site dedicated to helping kids realize their creative potential.

DogEared

National Geographic Kids—Digital Media

1145 17th Street NW

Washington, DC 20036

DogEared is a blog about books, with reviews, recommendations, opinions, and wish lists written by kids.

***Kenyon Review* Young Writers Workshop**

Finn House

102 West Wiggin Street

Kenyon College

Gambier, OH 43022

(740) 427-5208

Young Writers is an intensive two-week workshop for intellectually curious, motivated high school students who value writing. Its goal is to help students develop their creative and critical abilities with language—to become better, more productive writers and more insightful thinkers. The program is sponsored by the *Kenyon Review*, one of the country's preeminent literary magazines.

MidLink Magazine

SAS Campus Drive

Cary, NC 27513

(919) 531-2869

Web site: http://www.ncsu.edu/midlink

The mission of *MidLink* magazine is to highlight exemplary work from the most creative classrooms around the globe. All content must be original, must enhance learning, and must come directly from a classroom.

National Council of Teachers of English (NCTE)

Achievement Awards in Writing

1111 West Kenyon Road

Urbana, IL 61801-1096

Web site: http://www.ncte.org

The National Council of Teachers of English is devoted to improving the teaching and learning of English and the language arts at all levels of education. NCTE's Achievement Awards in Writing is a school-based writing program established in 1957 to encourage high school students in their writing and to recognize publicly some of the best student writers in the nation.

Weekly Reader Publishing

Weekly Reader's Student Publishing Contest

3001 Cindel Drive

Delran, NJ 08075

(800) 446-3355

Web site: http://www.weeklyreader.com

Weekly Reader's Student Publishing Contest honors the nation's best nonfiction writing by students in grades 3 through 12. Individual pieces, as well as print and online student publications, are eligible. Winners receive a free trip to Washington, D.C., plus other prizes.

Publishing and Posting

Below is a list of publications and Web sites that welcome submissions from young writers.

Merlyn's Pen

11 South Angell Street, Suite 301

Providence, RI 02906

(800) 247-2027

E-mail: merlyn@merlynspen.org

Web site: http://www.merlynspen.org

Skipping Stones

P.O. Box 3939

Eugene, OR 97403

(541) 342-4956

E-mail: info@skippingstones.org

Web site: http://www.skippingstones.org

Stone Soup

P.O. Box 83

Santa Cruz, CA 95063

(800) 447-4569

E-mail: editor@stonesoup.com

Web site: http://www.stonesoup.com

TeenInk

P.O. Box 30

Newton, MA 02461

(617) 964-6800

E-mail: editor@teenink.com

Web site: http://www.teenink.com

Teen Voices

80 Summer Street, Suite 300

Boston, MA 02110

(617) 426-5505

E-mail: teenvoices@teenvoices.com

Web site: http://www.teenvoices.com

Young Writers Project

Champlain Mill

20 Winooski Falls Way, Suite #4

Winooski, VT 05404

(802) 324-9537

Web site: http://youngwritersproject.org

Web Sites

Due to the changing nature of Internet links, Rosen Publishing has developed an online list of Web sites related to the subject of this book. This site is updated regularly. Please use this link to access the list:

http://www.rosenlinks.com/wlp/wai

FOR FURTHER READING

Benke, Karen. *Rip the Page!: Adventures in Creative Writing*. Boston, MA: Trumpeter Books, 2010.

DiPrince, Dawn, and Cheryl Miller Thurston. *Unjournaling: Daily Writing Exercises That Are NOT Personal, NOT Introspective, NOT Boring!* Fort Collins, CO: Cottonwood Press, 2006.

DiPrince, Dawn, and Cheryl Miller Thurston. *Yoga for the Brain: Daily Writing Stretches That Keep Minds Flexible and Strong*. Fort Collins, CO: Cottonwood Press, 2006.

Elliott, Rebecca S. *Painless Grammar*. Hauppauge, NY: Barron's Educational Series, 2006.

Fogarty, Mignon. *Grammar Girl Presents the Ultimate Writing Guide for Students*. New York, NY: Henry Holt, 2011.

Hanley, Victoria. *Seize the Story: A Handbook for Teens Who Like to Write*. Fort Collins, CO: Cottonwood Press, 2008.

Schwartz, Tina P. *Writing and Publishing: The Ultimate Teen Guide*. Lanham, MD: Scarecrow Press, 2010.

Singer, Jessica. *Stirring Up Justice: Writing and Reading to Change the World*. Portsmouth, NH: Heinemann, 2006.

INDEX

About the Authors

Roger Beutel is a writer who lives in Larchmont, New York.

Lauren Spencer is originally from California and now lives in New York City, where she teaches writing workshops in the public schools. She also writes lifestyle and music articles for magazines.

Photo Credits

Cover © www.istockphoto.com/zilli; pp. 4–5 © Kayte Deioma/ Photo Edit; p. 9 © Nancy Richmond/The Image Works; p. 16 © Michael Newman/Photo Edit; pp. 23, 49 Shutterstock; p. 28 © Spencer Grant/Photo Edit; p. 29 © www.istockphoto.com/ nicholas; p. 36 © Photononstop/SuperStock; p. 37 © www. istockphoto.com/Viktorita Yatskina; p. 45 Richard Sambrook.

Photo Researcher: Marty Levick

W9-DAI-617

I WANT TO KNOW

Was Sherlock Holmes Real?

Heather Moore Niver

Enslow Publishing
101 W. 23rd Street
Suite 240
New York, NY 10011
USA

enslow.com

Published in 2018 by Enslow Publishing, LLC.
101 W. 23rd Street, Suite 240, New York, NY 10011

Library of Congress Cataloging-in-Publication Data

Names: Niver, Heather Moore, author.
Title: Was Sherlock Holmes real? / Heather Moore Niver.
Description: New York, NY : Enslow Publishing, 2018. | Series: I want to know
 | Includes bibliographical references and index. | Audience: Grades 3-5.
Identifiers: LCCN 2017016541| ISBN 9780766091993 (library bound) | ISBN
 9780766093768 (pbk.) | ISBN 9780766093775 (6 pack)
Subjects: LCSH: Doyle, Arthur Conan, 1859-1930—Characters—Sherlock
 Holmes—Juvenile literature. | Holmes, Sherlock—Juvenile literature.
Classification: LCC PR4624 .N58 2018 | DDC 823/.8—dc23
LC record available at https://lccn.loc.gov/2017016541

Printed in China

To Our Readers: We have done our best to make sure all websites in this book were active and appropriate when we went to press. However, the author and the publisher have no control over and assume no liability for the material available on those websites or on any websites they may link to. Any comments or suggestions can be sent by email to customerservice@enslow.com.

Photo Credits: Cover ostill/Shutterstock.com; pp. 3, 25 Gillette/Hulton Archive/ Getty Images; pp. 4, 24 AF archive/Alamy Stock Photo; p. 7 adoc-photos/Corbis Historical/Getty Images; p. 9 Universal History Archive/Universal Images Group/ Getty Images; p. 11 J.M.E. Saxby/Wikimedia Commons/File:Joseph_Bell.jpg/CC BY 4.0 International; p. 12 MR. KHATAWUT/Shutterstock.com; p. 14 Swasdee/Shutterstock.com; p. 17 Materialscientist/Wikimedia Commons/File:Joseph_Bell.jpg/ CC BY 4.0 International; p. 19 Print Collector/Hulton Archive/Getty Images; p. 21 AVN Photo Lab/Shutterstock.com; p. 27 Collins93/Shutterstock.com; p. 28 Silver Screen Collection/Moviepix/Getty Images.

Contents

Actor Jeremy Brett is well known for playing Sherlock Holmes on British television for many years.

Chapter 1

· · · · · · · · · · ·

Man of Mystery

"Elementary!" With that single word, most people think of one character: Sherlock Holmes.

This famous **fictional** detective is very popular. Besides stories, Holmes has starred in plays and films. He has been played in 226 movies. Dozens of actors have played this character. Only Count Dracula has been in more films than Holmes. (The fanged fiend has been in 239 movies.) Sherlock Holmes became a model for many future detectives.

Imagine That!

Sherlock Holmes stars in four novels and fifty-six short stories written by Sir Arthur Conan Doyle.

A Study of Sherlock Holmes

Author Sir Arthur Conan Doyle's character first appeared in 1887. It was in the story *A Study in Scarlet*. Sherlock Holmes is introduced, and the relationship to his sidekick Dr. John H. Watson is explained. The two become friends. These partners solve mysteries together.

Holmes has black hair and gray eyes. His nose is "hawk-like." The detective is thin and stands more than 6 feet (183 centimeters) tall. He is in good physical shape.

Sherlock Holmes is a complicated character. The detective plays the violin quite well. He enjoys boxing and a Japanese sport known as Baritsu. He is also known to smoke a pipe.

He solves mysteries using logic, or reason. He also uses his powers of observation. In other words, he finds clues in what he sees. Holmes notices tiny details that other people don't see. He uses science, too.

Holmes is also good at disguises. This skill comes in handy. Sometimes Holmes wants to get information but doesn't want to be noticed. He dresses up like a religious

Arthur Conan Doyle was a doctor before he was "bitten" by the writing bug and decided to follow his passion for writing.

leader, a groom, and a French worker. Once he dressed up like a bookseller. Not even his own partner Dr. Watson could tell who he really was!

Doctor Conan Doyle

Arthur Ignatius Conan Doyle was born on May 22, 1859, in Edinburgh, Scotland. He went to the University of Edinburgh and graduated from the medical school in 1885. He worked as a doctor until 1891. Then Conan Doyle decided medical work was not for him. Lucky for detective story lovers, he became a writer instead.

Edgar Allan Poe and the Detective Story

Conan Doyle was not the first author to write about a detective. Edgar Allan Poe wrote about a detective hero in his short story "The Murders in the Rue Morgue" in

More Than Mysteries

Conan Doyle wrote things other than the Sherlock Holmes mysteries. He wrote historical novels. These are fictional stories that are based on history. He also wrote true articles about the military and some real-life crime mysteries.

1841. Poe definitely helped make the detective story popular. (The word "detective" was not yet used at the time Poe wrote!) Conan Doyle wrote that the **sleuth** "M. Dupin, had from boyhood been one of my heroes." Dupin appears in three stories by Poe. Conan Doyle was also a fan of Charles Dickens's detective stories.

Edgar Allan Poe is credited as the "father of detective fiction."

First Sherlock Story

Conan Doyle wrote his first Sherlock Holmes story in only three weeks. He was working as a doctor at the same time. *Beeton's Christmas Annual* agreed to publish *A Study in Scarlet,* but this first novel did not sell well.

Did Arthur Conan Doyle make up this quirky sleuth all on his own? Or was Sherlock Holmes a real-life detective? Yes and no. Like many fictional characters, Holmes was a result of a combination of **inspirations**.

Chapter 2

· · · · · · · · · · ·

The Real Doctor

Arthur Conan Doyle wrote *The Adventures of Sherlock Holmes* for "my old Teacher Joseph Bell, M.D." Dr. Joseph Bell had been his professor at the University of Edinburgh where Conan Doyle was studying medicine. Bell was a famous **forensic** scientist. He was also a top-notch teacher of surgery. Was Bell a model for Sherlock Holmes?

Imagine That!

When he wrote, Conan Doyle created the **solution** to his mystery first. Then he wrote his way to the beginning to create the story.

Sleuthing Symptoms

Bell had an unusual ability. He knew a person's **symptoms** almost immediately and could **diagnose** their illness. He could even figure out why

Dr. Joseph Bell had the amazing ability to diagnose patients at a glance.
He became a model for the character Sherlock Holmes.

they were sick. Conan Doyle wrote that Dr. Bell "would sit … and diagnose the people as they came in, before they even opened their mouths. He would tell them details of their past life, and hardly would he ever make a mistake." Holmes says, "You know my method. It is founded on the observation of **trifles**." Holmes noticed tiny details that others might miss. For example, he would note when mud on a boot was the color only found in a certain part of town.

Small details, such as an unusual color of mud on someone's boots, could help investigators pinpoint a specific place and solve a crime.

Bell and Holmes also look a little bit alike. Both have "sharp and piercing" gray eyes. They both have narrow, hooked noses.

Joe Bell

Joseph "Joe" Bell was born in Edinburgh on December 2, 1837. His family was very religious. He referred to the Bible all his life. Young Joe also loved nature. He was a good student and an athlete.

Many of Bell's teachers at Edinburgh Academy were violent. Physical punishment was much more common at that time. But D'Arcy Wentworth Thompson was kind. He treated students with respect. Bell always tried to be the same kind of teacher.

Bell graduated from the University of Edinburgh in 1859. He was twenty-one years old. His career took off right away. Eventually Bell became a famous forensic scientist, teaching at the University of Edinburgh. He wrote textbooks and medical papers throughout his life.

Bell graduated from the University of Edinburgh in Scotland and went on to teach there. This is where he and Conan Doyle met.

Detecting Differences

Sherlock Holmes is not just Joseph Bell with a different name. Conan Doyle may have used Bell's talents in his stories, but he also used his imagination.

Bell was known to be a thoughtful and caring man. Everyone liked him—students and other professors. Everyone knew him as "Joe."

Sherlock Holmes has a prickly personality. Many people do not like him. He also has some unfortunate addictions to tobacco and other drugs. Bell was not known to use any of these things.

Conan Doyle only used Bell's genius when he wrote about Holmes. The rest was all made up for a good story. "My Dear Dr. Bell," Conan Doyle wrote. "It is most certainly to you that I owe Sherlock Holmes, although in the stories I have the advantage of being able to place him in all sorts of dramatic situations."

Chapter 3

· · · · · · · · · · ·

Doyle and the Detective

Not everyone is convinced that Dr. Joseph Bell is a perfect fit for Holmes's real-life model. Conan Doyle probably used **characteristics** from other people he knew to create his detective. He may have even used himself! It sure makes for a good mystery.

What About Littlejohn?

Sir Henry Littlejohn was a famous forensic scientist. And he may have been another model for Sherlock Holmes. Littlejohn was a surgeon for the Scottish police. Littlejohn was famous for analyzing, or examining, crime scenes and victims. He was also an expert witness for some

Another famous forensic scientist named Sir Henry Littlejohn was a whiz at examining crime scenes and victims.

well-known criminal cases. He and Joseph Bell cracked some famous cases together. Littlejohn taught classes at the University of Edinburgh, but it was after Conan Doyle had graduated. Conan Doyle would have been well aware of his work.

Doyle the Detective?

Conan Doyle once contacted Scotland Yard, the London police. He told them about a man who was convicted of killing a lot of horses and cows. Conan Doyle proved to them that the man's eyesight was terrible. It was so bad, there was no way he could have killed the animals.

In 1916, Conan Doyle was on another case. He tried to help an Irish official named Sir Roger Casement. In this case, he was not successful. This case was an inspiration for his writing. Lord John Roxton in *The Lost World* was based on Casement.

Imagine That!

Jerome Caminada was another Holmes inspiration for Conan Doyle. Caminada was a police officer in Manchester, England. He was known for his excellent disguises, just like Sherlock Holmes. He also had a **nemesis** named Bod Horridge.

"HOLMES GAVE ME A SKETCH OF THE EVENTS."

Sherlock Holmes (*right*) and Dr. Watson chat about their latest case on a train in an illustration for the story "The Adventure of Silver Blaze."

What's With Watson?

Dr. John Watson is Holmes's most trusted partner. For a while, they are even roommates. Some people feel

Elementary!

When Holmes states, "Elementary," he is usually talking to Dr. Watson. Sherlock Holmes is known for saying, "Elementary, my dear Watson." But this line never appears in any of the stories. Holmes says, "Oh this is elementary, my dear fellow."

that Dr. Watson is based on Conan Doyle himself. In the stories, Watson always writes about Sherlock Holmes's cases. He is the narrator, or storyteller, in most of the Sherlock Holmes stories. Of course, Watson and Conan Doyle were both doctors, too.

What's With the Hat?

The Sherlock Holmes stories were originally published in *Strand* magazine. Artist Sydney Paget was the illustrator. The iconic Holmes look includes a strange hat called a **deerstalker**. A deerstalker has a brim on both the front and the back. It also has earflaps. The deerstalker is never mentioned in any of the books. Paget might have chosen the deerstalker based on a general description in the book. Holmes wears a traveling cap with earflaps.

Illustrations by Sidney Paget showed Holmes wearing the striking deerstalker hat, which came to be associated with Holmes.

Paget's images were so good that nearly everyone thinks of Holmes wearing the deerstalker! Paget may have used his own brother Walter as a model as he drew Holmes.

The Name Game

Sir Arthur Conan Doyle may have named his characters for people he knew. Holmes's last name may have come from American doctor Oliver Wendell Holmes. His first name could be related to a violinist who was popular at the time, Alfred Sherlock. There was a real-life Dr. John Watson, who was a physician, too.

Chapter 4

· · · · · · · · · · ·

Holmes Comes to Life

Sherlock Holmes has been brought to life many times on stage and screen. Actors including Basil Rathbone, Peter Cushing, Jeremy Brett, Robert Downey Jr., and Benedict Cumberbatch have played the sly sleuth. But the first was William Hooker Gillette. Gillette played Holmes onstage. His characterization of Sherlock Holmes was very effective. Many of the classic characteristics we associate with Holmes today came from Gillette.

Imagine That!

William Gillette helped create a Sherlock Holmes group. It's called the Baker Street Irregulars. (Baker Street is where Holmes and Watson lived.) This group is still active today.

Actor Robert Downey Jr. plays a modern version of the quirky Sherlock Holmes in several movies.

Sherlock Holmes Onstage

In the late 1890s, Conan Doyle wrote a play about Holmes. William Hooker Gillette was a famous actor at the time. He read the play and liked it. He asked Conan Doyle's permission to change Holmes's character a little bit. Conan Doyle agreed.

Gillette worked on the play himself. He drastically changed Holmes. Conan Doyle didn't seem to mind. When he saw the changes, he said, "It's good to see the old chap again."

Some of the costumes William Hooker Gillette wore as
Holmes are still associated with the detective today.

The play went onstage in 1901. It was performed in London, England, at the Lyceum Theater. Critics gave it bad reviews, but the public loved it! Gillette's portrayal inspired future actors who played Holmes, too.

The Pipe, the Robe, and the Hat (Again)

Gillette was one of the most popular actors to play Holmes. Some of the clothes he wore to play him are still connected with Holmes today. Holmes smoked a straight pipe in the novels and stories. Gillette used a long, swooping pipe in his performances. It is called a calabash. This style may have been more comfortable on his jaw. It allowed him to keep the pipe in his mouth while talking, too.

Holmes also wore a long dressing gown, or a kind of robe. In the books, Holmes wears a simple robe. Gillette wore one that was much fancier. Gillette also wore a deerstalker hat.

Basil Rathbone is best known for first playing Holmes in movies. He wore the hat, too. He also smoked a pipe and used a spyglass. Holmes does use a spyglass sometimes in the Conan Doyle stories.

Gillette Castle

William Gillette's acting career was successful. He made so much money that he was able to design and build his own home in East Haddam, Connecticut. It came to be called Gillette Castle. (He did not call it a castle, though.) It even has its own miniature railroad. In 2014, a silent film, *Sherlock Holmes,* was found in a film archive in France. It is the only known movie to star Gillette. It was eventually shown in Gillette Castle.

Good-bye Holmes?

In 1893, Conan Doyle decided he wanted to stop writing about Holmes. In the story "The Final Problem," Holmes and his **nemesis** Professor Moriarty fall off a cliff. Readers were outraged! Twenty thousand people canceled their subscription to *Strand* magazine. Even the British royal family expressed sadness. Finally, the author gave in. In 1903,

This 1939 movie poster features Basil Rathbone as Sherlock Holmes on the silver screen.

Conan Doyle published *The Adventure of the Empty House*. He wrote about how the detective managed to survive the fall. Sherlock was back! He wrote about Sherlock Holmes for almost the rest of his life.

Words to Know

characteristic A special feature that makes someone or something stand out from the rest.

deerstalker A hat with brims on both ends and earflaps, often associated with Sherlock Holmes.

diagnose To explain an illness or problem.

fictional Made up.

forensic Related to using the scientific method to investigate crime.

inspiration Something that causes a feeling or action.

nemesis An enemy or rival, usually over a long period of time.

sleuth A detective.

solution The answer to a problem or mystery.

symptom Something that shows the presence of an illness or disease.

trifle Something small and seemingly unimportant.

Further Reading

Books

Doyle, Arthur Conan. *The Adventures of Sherlock Holmes.* Richmond, England: Alma Classics, 2016.

Doyle, Arthur Conan. *How Watson Learned the Trick: A Sherlock Holmes Story*. Somerville, MA: Candlewick Press, 2015.

Doyle, Arthur Conan, and Tony Evans. *A Study in Scarlet*. Stroud, Gloucestershire, UK: Real Reads, 2013.

Klinger, Leslie S., David Stuart Davies, and Barry Forshaw. *The Sherlock Holmes Book*. New York, NY: DK Penguin Random House, 2015.

Websites

Arthur Conan Doyle

arthurconandoyle.com/characters.html

Learn more about Holmes, Watson, and other characters in Arthur Conan Doyle's stories.

BBC

bbc.co.uk/guides/zcx2hv4

Learn how to think like Sherlock Holmes!

The Sherlock Holmes Museum

sherlock-holmes.co.uk

Check out a quiz, video, and more about Sherlock Holmes.

Index